AF084244

CATNIP

A play by
James Ernest

Published by Playdead Press 2014

© James Ernest 2014

James Ernest has asserted his rights under the Copyright, Design and Patents Act, 1988, to be identified as the author of this work.

A CIP catalogue record for this book is available from the British Library.

ISBN 978-1-910067-05-5

Caution

All rights whatsoever in this play are strictly reserved and application for performance should be sought through the author before rehearsals begin. No performance may be given unless a license has been obtained.

This book is sold subject to the condition that it shall not by way of trade or otherwise, be lent, resold, hired out, or otherwise circulated without the publisher's prior consent in any form of binding or cover other than that in which it is published and without a similar condition including this condition being imposed on the subsequent purchaser.

Printed by BPUK

Playdead Press
www.playdeadpress.com

For my Mother.

Foreword

The subject is Love.

You may totally disagree with what I write, which is perfectly fine, because what I write down is drawn from my own personal experiences.

I try to appreciate what I'm holding, the moment that I'm living in, but I find it difficult.
My mind is regularly hovering over the future, what I need to do, what I want to happen, what will probably happen and what actions I can take to make a situation better.
But when you experience love, all you care about is the now.
That is why it is so addictive and so beautiful.
It's the only thing that forces us to truly live and truly care about that moment we are living in.

That feeling of elevation.
That bliss is what each of us live for and that is the foundation for hope.
The hope that we find someone who will love us until the day we die.
Someone that will make us their everything, their one main reason for living.

Essentially, we learn how to love from our families.
We are taught how we should treat one another from our Mother or our Grandmother.
I was fortunate enough to have the best tuition.
Some are not as fortunate.

Some have never received a single dose of it.
Some are brought up with a sordid idea of love.

So, they don't have much to live for, but to hate, to destroy and to corrupt others.
They do not possess a bone in their body that emanates the feeling of true love.

If love didn't exist in our lives, somehow or somewhere, neither would we.
We would nothing more than a cracked shell, writhing in agony.
We would not be able to empathise
We would be incapable of any sort of human affection.

Now and then, the love that we give to another is taken, abused then torn.
The repercussions of this is damaging, it pushes us to lie to ourselves, we then believe we are strong enough, we are certain that we need no one else.
We stop receiving.
We create barriers, huge walls, gigantic burrows and underground pathways.
This is because we are afraid to be left alone without love or without the hope.

We need to stop now.

We need to stop manifesting and obsessing and we need to climb out of those craters.
We need to stop fabricating and decorating.
We need to live in this moment.
For this moment deserves to be lived in.

I urge you, if you haven't already, watch *The Great Dictator*. Charlie Chaplin is a beautiful man that articulates this point far better than I.

I hope you enjoy the show.

Please come and talk to me after the performance, I will be more than happy to hear your thoughts.

James Ernest - December 2013

James Ernest
Playwright and Director

In 2012, James Ernest's first play, *The 8th Wave* was shortlisted for the Soho Young Writers' Award. The play was performed at The Tristan Bates and later, the production transferred to The Space, where it gained critical acclaim from several well-established critics. This play was also published by Playdead Press.

CATNIP was developed on the Royal Court Young Writers' Programme in spring 2013. The play came into the top 75 scripts category (out of 800 scripts) for the Verity Bargate Award 2013.
After several rewrites and a couple of readings with professional actors, James felt it was time to get the script up onto its feet and start constructing a quality production with it.

He would also like to thank the following people, for if it wasn't for them, this production would not have been possible.

Disturbance RTN
East 15 Acting School
IdeasTap
The Rich Mix
The Royal Court Theatre

CATNIP was first performed at The Rich Mix in February 2013.

This script was published during rehearsals, so it may vary from the production itself.

Original score and lyrics by Anthony Stephen Springall
Additional Lyrics by James Ernest

Original Cast
In order of appearance

Roger Parkins
Derrick

Roger is an actor and a musician. He is a part of the band Archean Soundtrack, the group has recently returned from their National Tour. He is currently acting in *Tristram Shandy* at the Tabard Theatre. Previous credits include *Next Time I'll Sing to You* (The Orange Tree), *Sherlock Homes* (Leicester Square Theatre) and *Pirates of Penzance* (Tabard Theatre).

Kes Gill-Martin
David

Kes is an actor, poet and co-founder of Hit The Ground Theatre Company. Roles as an actor include Hamlet in *Hamlet* (Jorvik Theatre), Jaw in *After Cease to Exist* (Feature Film, Grand Independent) and Montano in *Othello* (Bussey Building). His work across genres has led him to a range of venues including Rich Mix, Free Word Centre and Southbank Centre.

Anna Swan
Julie

Anna Swan trained at East 15 Acting School. Anna is relishing the challenge of playing Julie and has thoroughly enjoyed working with such a talented cast and creative team.

Lewis Allcock
Stephen

Lewis Allcock was born in Blackburn, Lancashire, and trained at East 15. Theatre work includes *La Ronde* (Tristan Bates Theatre), *Tristram Shandy* (Tabard Theatre) and *Woyzeck* (Scene Productions). Film work includes the feature *Nightmare Hunters* (Black Rock Films) and *The Turn* (Mango Films), amongst other corporate work.

Robyn Keynes
Producer

Robyn attended the prestigious Stage One New Producers Workshop in 2012 and NSDF Management Training Programme in 2013, where she worked alongside festival director Michael Brazier to producer the final night awards ceremony. As well as freelance work she was Assistant Producer at Independent Productions, working on two UK sell-out tours; the Time Out Critics' Choice show, Boy in A Dress and The Bear in a co-production with Improbable. She is passionate about new writing and aims to bring bold, original work to both the commercial and subsidized sectors.

Lily Levin
Assistant director

Lily Levin is a passionate actor and theatre maker who was asked to assistant direct Catnip with its writer, James Ernest. Ernest and Levin have a history of working together including training rigorously together at East15 Acting School. After going to the Edinburgh Fringe with The Alchemist's *Humans Inc*, Levin is also currently redeveloping said show as an actor and co-deviser. Levin is also working up the courage to book her third stand up gig.

Anthony Stephen Springall
Composer/Lyricist/Musical Director

Anthony has written over 200 songs for a variety of productions. To date, he has written two full length musicals & underscores music for theatre and short films. He graduated in 2012 from East 15 Acting School and now writes mainly for his theatre company The Alchemist.

Setting

The play is set in several different locations.

A community centre.
A traditional semi-detached house.
The YMCA.
The local park.

These locations are all a part of a little village called Swinton in South Yorkshire.

The director may choose to place the scenes in other environments in the village, this is perfectly fine.

Characters

Derrick is in his late thirties.

David is late teens.

Julie is in her forties.

Stephen is between late twenties and early thirties.

These are my preferred ages for the cast, but the director may want to use younger or indeed older actors for the parts. This is understandable.

Notes

- Character interrupted, lost in thought or unable to express themselves, loss of words.

One.

Derrick: The glitter of hope.
That is what brings us together, here, today, in this room.

What is that dark, quivering glow that surrounds us?
What is creating that fearsome creature, lurking tightly in the very corners of your shadow?
You cannot see it.
But you can feel it, suffocating and invading.

We all have secrets.
We all bear unspeakable thoughts and feelings.
We all repress.
We all isolate.
We don't all have friends and family that are willing to support us.

We are here to listen to one another.
To make friends.
To laugh and to cry.
To share stories.

We will play games.
Nobody has played these sorts of games before.

I will not tell you what to do.
But, I will hint at how to play them.
This will help us bond.

Depth.

We are all on the same side.
That is what we have in common.
Isn't it?

Welcome to Man Speak.

Are you cold David?

David: I'm fine.
I have a jumper on.

Derrick: Do you wear vests?

David: Yes.

Derrick: Good.

How often?

David: Now and then.

Derrick: Are you wearing one now?

David: Yes.

Derrick: Did you wear one yesterday?

David: I don't think so.

Derrick: We are not going to get anywhere David if your answers are inaccurate.

David: Sorry.

Derrick: You're forgiven.
Now think.

David: Thursday –

Derrick: David.

David: I didn't wear a vest.

Derrick: And why not?

David: I never wear one when I ride my bike.

Derrick: I see.

Brilliant.
We're making progress.

David: Wednesday I wore one.

Derrick: You're rushing ahead.

David: I'm sorry.

Derrick: You're forgiven.

So, did you wear a vest on Wednesday?

David: Yes.

Derrick: Was it cotton?

David: Yes.

Derrick: Details.

	Was it One hundred percent cotton?
David:	Yes, it was.
Derrick:	Good. One hundred percent. Well done.
	So, I'm trying to understand something David. Perhaps you could help me? You are pretty confidant, aren't you?
	David? Would that be an accurate assumption?
	Would that be viable?
David:	Confidence –
Derrick:	I don't think I've had somebody come here, with so much – Why did you come here David? What made you?
David:	It doesn't –
Derrick:	I think the answer is pretty simple. I'll tell you why, shall I?
David:	Confidence doesn't –
Derrick:	You have come here to reveal something. Something that you couldn't possibility admit to those that are close to you.

                    You are unable to communicate with those
                    that love you.

                    So, what do you think we need to do?

David: Confidence doesn't exist.
                    Insecurity does, insecurity exists.

Derrick: We need to dig David.
                    We need to discover.
                    The truth is what we need.
                    But revealing this truth is the difficult
                    part.
                    That comes with the trust.

                    Once we have trust and you have revealed
                    the truth, and once you have accepted this
                    truth, we then move on.

Music begins to play

David: I think I have an addiction.

Derrick: You think?

David: I have an addiction.

Derrick: What are you into?

Addicted to them all

David: Spanking, Felching, Cream Pie.
Licking chicks, Brown neckties.
Angry Dragon up against a wall, I'm addicted to them all.

Sluts and Porn go hand in hand.
Girls drowning in their orange tans.
Polling wank in the village hall, it's a vote for Liberal.

My Obsession with dogging is becoming an issue.
Lurking in the dark with a packet of tissues.
I need to dig my way out of this hole
I'm feeling like a mole, mole, mole, mole, mole, mole, mole, mole.

Don't write this down.

Derrick:
No.

Never.
I will never take notes.

Never ink, we do not use the ink in here.
Ink is for crosswords.

Now, tell me about your childhood.

All:

Red Tube, Skeezy, Spank wire.
Man hub, Jizz club, no man's attire.
Will he rise or will he fall?
Being addicted to them all.

Two.

Derrick has a newspaper on his lap and a pen in his hand
He is trying to solve a crossword
Julie is wearing a pair of pink fluffy slippers and a raunchy piece of lingerie covered by a silk robe

Julie: I've been asked to write an article on domestic abuse.
It's really current.
Very now.

Derrick: Castrate?

Julie: Everybody is hunting for the biggest story.
All the papers are fighting for it.
The editors are salivating over the very thought of it.

Derrick: No, that can't be right, no.

Julie: So, I'm keeping my eyes and ears open from now on.
We've all been told that.
To 'Be aware.'

Derrick: Six letters, not 8.

Julie: Linda popped round today.
Her career is really taking off Derrick.
I still can't believe she's a soap star.
It hasn't sunk in.

Derrick: She's hardly a soap star.

Julie: How can you say that?
She's been on Emmerdale.

Derrick: She was an extra.

Julie: She had lines.

Derrick: Three.
Eleven words.
We watched it four times, so I counted.

"Are these yours?"
"No?"
And, "I can't find who they belong to."

The woman is not a soap star.

Julie: She's very successful for her age.

Derrick: How old is she?

Julie: She's thirty two.

Derrick: Is she?

Julie: It took that Judy Dench thirty three years to get famous.
That film made her, Educating something or other.

I didn't like it very much.
We prefer Mama Mia don't we?
We like her in that.

	Linda looks a little bit like Judy. Don't you think? It's the eyes. Don't you think?
Derrick:	Julie Walters.
Julie:	Who?
Derrick:	That's who you mean.
Julie:	Do I?
Derrick:	Julie was in Educating Rita, not Judy.
Julie:	Was it? Are you sure? Anyway, Linda told me, she's recently been cast to play a young maid. She said that's her 'Casting type.' 'Young maid' or 'Prostitute.' I'm so proud of her. Look where she is. Emmerdale last week, Downton Abbey next. That's one of our favorites isn't it? Oh, 'Young maid two.' She does look twenty five. Looks after herself she does.

Julie walks over to the window

Julie:	She's very beautiful. Don't you think? I wished I looked twenty five. I try. I bought some anti-wrinkle cream last week from Boots. They won't budge.
Derrick:	It ends with a 'P.'
Julie:	Derrick!
Derrick:	I'm listening. Come away from the window. You're naked.
Julie:	Hardly.
Derrick:	You're hardly wearing –
Julie:	Do you think people can see my bottom half if I do this?
Derrick:	Julie, come away from the window.
Julie:	I'll close the curtains shall I?

She closes the curtains and walks over to the mirror

Julie:	She had those blonde highlights in her hair. She came straight from the hair dressers. Little ringlets.

	Forties style. Downton Abbey style. That is so adorable, don't you think?
Derrick:	Slipup.
Julie:	I always wanted to be that beautiful. Born with beauty. Derrick, do you think I could be a lesbian?
Derrick:	I don't think you'd be a very good lesbian.
Julie:	Why's that?
Derrick:	You said don't like vagina.
Julie:	You're right. I don't like vagina. It's an acquired taste.
Derrick:	Have you tried it before?
Julie:	Everybody has tried their own, haven't they?
Derrick:	I haven't.
Julie:	It's a natural thing Derrick. It is perfectly normal to explore. Linda asked me to join her on a cookery course.

Derrick: Didn't you tell me she was great in the kitchen?

Julie: She is.
She made us that spaghetti Bolognese that time.
Do you remember?
She's great.
It turns out she wants to learn how to cook the 'Mediterranean Cuisine.'

Derrick: That's what the course is for?
'The Mediterranean Cuisine?'

Julie: I told her we don't eat Mediterranean food.
I told her we don't like it.

Derrick: We've never tried it.

Julie: We have, two years ago.
We only went there once, we never went back.

Derrick: Braithwaite's?
That wasn't a Mediterranean buffet.
That was Thai.

Julie: Are you sure?

Derrick: I'm positive.

Julie: Who'd name a Thai restaurant Braithwaite's?

Derrick: Who would name a Mediterranean restaurant Braithwaite's?

Julie: It's possible.

Derrick: Is it?

Julie: It is.

Derrick: Really?

Julie: Yes Derrick.

Derrick: Are you going?

Julie: I was going to go, I was sold.
Until, Linda told me that in me in the 'Mediterranean cuisine,' they remove the skins from all of their cucumbers.

Derrick: Really?

Julie: I told her I thought it was silly.
Apparently the skin of the cucumber gives you indigestion.

Derrick: You don't get indigestion.

Julie: I know, that's what I told her.
I said that my digestion is just fine.
That is why I said no.
I told her my diet is just fine and I don't need to alter it.

I don't want to alter it.

                    I like it how it is.
                    I'm keeping it the same.

Derrick: Good.

Stephen enters
He takes out a packet of matches and begins to light
the candles that are scattered around the room

Julie: She told me some more juicy information about that burglary. They still haven't caught that bloke.
                    Didn't get anything back after she put it on Crime Watch.
                    She said he's been visiting a lot of houses.

                    I bought some handcuffs, today.
                    Just in case we have to do one of those, what do you call it?
                    Citizen's arrest?
                    She showed me the CCTV footage.
                    He didn't know they had cameras.
                    No idea.
                    Very clever, we should get some.
                    Valid piece of evidence.
                    What do you think?

                    I had to go in one of those sexy shops at Donny.
                    The woman behind the counter gave me a little smile when I put them on the counter.
                    I had to explain.
                    I would hate for her to get the wrong impression.

>   I looked at the clothes in there too.
>   Tried on a few sets.
>   Just for a giggle.
>   A bit of fun.
>   I liked it.

Julie opens her silk robe

>   I bought this.
>   Do you like it?
>   Derrick?
>
>   Derrick?
>
>   Derrick!

Derrick: Yes, great, yes.

Julie: Did you know one of those foxes stole some of Linda's lingerie?
               One moment it was on her line.
               The next, gone.

Stephen exits

Julie: I'll share something with you.
               Linda told me, she thinks they are starting to invade.
               There becoming ruthless Derrick.
               She believes, as the time has passed, the foxes have started recognizing things, you know certain qualities that they fear about themselves.
               Linda believes these things, them qualities are in us Derrick, humans.

	The foxes have started to accept it.

                    The foxes have started to accept it.
                    Accept who they really are.
                    They are becoming unafraid of us.

Derrick: What do foxes want with laundry?

Julie: Bedding.
They're very intelligent.

Derrick: Did she see it?

Julie: No, she didn't, she heard the fox.
It was in the middle of the night.
Foxes are unpredictable.
She says they are 'Pissed off.'
They feel angry.
And now they are coming back.
Trying their hardest to take control.
Like they once did Derrick.

Oh, it was ever so nice to speak to her.
She's coming around in the morning for breakfast and a cup of tea.
It's all arranged.

Derrick: What time?

Julie: Eleven.

Derrick: That's brunch.
Not breakfast.

What time was today then?

Julie: Half eleven today.

Because of her appointment at the hairdressers.

Now.

Julie takes off her robe, turns the bedside lamp off and gets into bed

Julie: OK.

Can you?

Stephen enters again, with David

Derrick: Of Course.

Derrick puts his head underneath the covers and begins to lick

David: Will you look at this.

You've got your kitchen.
You've got your bedroom, shower, and a bloody toilet.
It's an en-fucking-suite!

Stephen: I'm lucky.

David: I'm impressed.
What's this place called again?

Stephen: YMCA.

David: Fuck me.
How much do you pay?

Stephen: Eleven pound.

David: Eleven pound a day?

Stephen: A week.

David: You're joking me.

Stephen: Breakfast included.

David: You're pulling my bloody leg.
Sausage?
Egg?
Hash bastard brown?

Stephen: I'm very lucky.

David: You are, you're right there.
You are right there –
What's your name again?

Stephen: Stephen.

David: Steve.
I want to make something as clear Steve.
I'm not queer.

Stephen: You're not here for sex?

David: No, not here for that sort of thing.

Stephen: Right.

David: I was given some advice you see, someone told me to come here.

	To you.
Stephen:	Derrick.
David:	He said you do 'Role play.'
Stephen:	I can do that.
David:	So you do do that? Because if you don't, I will have to find somewhere else to go, see someone else.
Stephen:	I do that.
David:	Great. Perfect. He sent me to two other lads before you. They didn't work out though. I didn't believe them. I walked in, looked at them and walked straight back out.
Stephen:	Right.
David:	But I think you'll do. I think I'll believe you.
Stephen:	That's good.
David:	You don't have any seats though, any chairs? You've got a table, but no bloody chairs? How does that work?

Stephen: Does this involve sitting down?

David: It did, yes.
I wanted a chair.

       The floor's filthy.
When was the last time you swept?

Stephen: Is that going to be a problem?

David: A big one, yes.
You see, he was very clean my Dad.

Stephen: Your –

David: He was immaculate.
An immaculate man.
He worked in the steel works.
He'd get home, but he couldn't do anything until the oil and shit was washed off his body.

Stephen: We could use the bed?

David: I didn't imagine him sat on the bed.
He would sit on a chair.
Fucking hell Steve.

       You'll have to sit on the floor.

       Have you got a broom?
A brush?

Stephen: I have newspaper.

David: He didn't read.
He was illiterate.

Stephen: For the floor.
To cover up the mess.

David: —
I'll do the floor, cover up the mess.
You get yourself into these.

David gives Stephen a plastic bag with a pile of his father's clothes in it
Stephen begins to change into the clothes
David begins to cover the floor in newspaper

Stephen: These jeans are big.

David: He wore them big, with the braces holding them up.

David takes out a small bottle of Calvin Crave and sprays Stephen with it vigorously
David notices a scar on Stephen's chest as he is getting changed
He pauses, and then he carries on spraying

David: My mentor says this will help.
He says it's an exercise that will 'Fix' me.
'Better than pills' he told me.
He says it will 'Cure.'

Stephen: Did he?

David: I have a problem you see.
Something I can't control.

Stephen: You –

David: I'm trying to, you know, control it.

It's aggression.

Stephen: And you think this is going to help?

David: Try everything once.

Except scat.
Nobody likes to get shit on.

Stephen: No.

David: It's quite cold in this room.

Stephen: No radiators.

David: You must freeze in the winter.

Stephen: No, I wear warm clothes.

David: Don't you shiver?

Stephen: Never.

David: What about in your sleep?

Stephen: No.

David: How do you know?
Don't you wear vests?

Stephen: I never shiver.

David: How do you dry your clothes?

Stephen: We have another room for that.
Washing, drying.

David: There's the catch.
Electricity?

Stephen: Candles and daylight.

David: How do you watch porn?

Julie: OH.

Stephen: I don't.

David: Fucking hell.
I have to watch it at least six a day.
I have to cum at least six times a day, otherwise I get frustrated.

Stephen: Right.

David: Sexual frustration is a fucker.
Sometimes watching porn and having a wank just isn't enough though.
So, I turn to my girlfriend, now and then, to help me out.

She doesn't always want to though, sometimes she can't.
And I know it's not her fault, I understand that.
But it frustrates me, her saying no.
That rejection agitates me.

	It pumps up inside of me, It devours me, takes control. I get angry and I explode.
Stephen:	What do you do?
David:	I beat her. And I can't help it.
Stephen:	You won't –
David:	But when I do shoot, it calms me down. Once I've had that feeling of – Of – You know. I turn back into my good old self. Derrick told me, these problems, that frustration, that agitation, that anger, it 'Derives from my childhood.' There are things in my past, in my childhood where I felt oppressed or – 'Suppression when suppressed is expressed in different ways.' He told me this is the way to sort them out. Must go back to the 'Root of the problems.'
Stephen:	Have you got the money?
David:	Yes, I have, sorry.

Stephen: Don't apologise.

David: Twenty, forty, sixty.

Stephen: Five.

David: Yes, sorry.

Sixty-Five.

Stephen: Right.
So, what's the situation?

David: I've drawn a picture.
Here, look.

Stephen: Right.

David: I've always been good at design.

When I was younger, about six or seven, I would sit in my room and design dens.
Detailed I was too.
Me and some lads had our very own tree.
Made it into our den.
In it, we had cushions, old sofas, and blue plastic sheeting to stop the rain coming through.

Stephen: Who's that?

David: My Dad.
That's the bed.

Stephen: So, what's the situation?

David: You will start in the other room.
It'll have to be the toilet.

I'm in my room, in my bed.
I wake up.
Not because of the arguing, but because of my legs.
I had leg ache.
Really fucking painful stuff.
Went to the hospital once, had a fucking X-ray.
Turns out to be growing pains.
I was in tears.

But you're in the other room.
You've just found out Mum was shagging some other bloke.
You can't hear me crying.
So, I begin to scream for you, to help.
I scream louder and louder, grabbing holding of my legs, I hit them a few times, I remember that.

You hear me, you come into my room and you look at me for a second.
I asked you to make the pain go away.
I ask for your help.

He didn't though, he left.
He left the house and he jumped in front of a train.
I had tracks near my house.
At the back of my house.

Killed himself.

| | But I don't want that to happen, in the situation.
That's not the situation I want.
I want you to sit down on my floor, beside my bed and I want you to tell me a story until I fall asleep. |
|---|---|
| **Stephen:** | What shall I – |
| **David:** | How'd you get your scar? |
| **Stephen:** | My – |
| **David:** | Your, on your chest, upside down T shape?
I've got one on my ass.
It was the gym that did mine.
How'd you get yours? |
| **Stephen:** | Car accident.
Ended up in a hospital.
Heart transplant. |
| **David:** | Shit.
Can I touch it? |
| **Julie:** | OHH. |

David places his hand on Stephen's chest

Stephen:	An average male heart beats two billion, seven hundred million times in its entire lifetime.

David: Shit.
You're not fucking about are you?
Not messing.

Is it ticking?

Stephen: It ticks.

David: Never met anyone like you before.

When you woke up, did you feel like a different person?

You know, you were unconscious, right?
You can't remember the operation.
You saw the results, the evidence, the scars.
So you weren't present in your body.
You were comatose.
So, you were living in your head, your brain, right, and you lived there.

They take your heart out, and they give you a new one.
A different one, somebody else's.
Now this heart becomes a part of you.
Keeps you alive.

The doctors gave you a gift.
The surgeons, the fucking NHS.
They gave you another chance.

There was love in that heart.
Kindness and generosity in it.
That's why you survived.

                        So, when you woke, did you feel like
                        yourself?
                        Or did you feel different?

Stephen: It changed me, yes.

Julie: OHHH!

Thump
Bedside table lamp on
Derrick appears from underneath the covers

Julie: Did you hear that?
                      They're at it again.
                      They've been at it a lot recently.

Derrick: At what?

Julie walks to the wall and places her ear against it

Julie: Linda and Andrew, arguing a lot.
                      Pass me a cup.

Derrick: Leave them to it.

Julie: I will not 'Leave them to it.'
                      Linda is my best friend.

                      I heard them last night too, eleven it was,
                      they woke me up.

                      Pass me a cup.

Derrick passes Julie the coffee cup that was sitting on the bedside table

She places it against the wall

Derrick: Would you like a cup of coffee?

Julie: Can you go and make it?

David: I like stories, always have done.
My dad would sit me on his knee.
Usually it was before bedtime.

He told me stories about his arm.
He only had one, he lost the other working in the steel works.
He told me stories of how he lost it, lots of different versions.
After a while I forgot which one was the real story.

I have a photo of us playing baseball when I was four.
Keep it in my wallet, he stays in there.

Almost never take it out.

Julie: Oh!
He just called her a bitch.

Three.

Derrick: Time.
I always arrive at my appointments ten minutes early.
Sometimes even earlier than that.
I need those ten minutes to prepare and to clear my mind.
You can never clear your mind fully.
There are always little things wriggling about somewhere in the brain.
But I try, my very best to clear it as much as I possibly can.
I exhale.

I think over previous sessions.
I think about ways in which we could progress, together.

I will never give you advice.
Instead, I will hint at what you need to do.
These subtle hints will lead to progress.
If you take them on board that is.

We need to work together.
That is why I take my ten minutes.
Prepare to feel open and willing.
Appear hopeful, helpful and kind.

We must trust each other one hundred percent.
Look each other in the eyes.
That's the most important thing.

| | The truth comes from looking at each other's eyes. |
| | You did see Stephen? |

David: Yes.

Derrick: The eyes David.

David: Yes.

Derrick: Did he sort you out?

David: I'm seeing him again on Friday.

Derrick: Oh good.
He's a good employee.
Sorts people out.
My friends.

I hope you don't mind me calling you that. I would hate for you to think I was crossing the professional boundary.
My professional walls?

David: I don't –

Derrick: Oh good.
Ok then.

We're making progress, I can tell.

How much are you paying him?

David: Sixty-Five.

Derrick: OK, good.

Julie: I was only popping round to say hello.
We haven't seen each other in some time so I thought I would pop round.
I would hate her to think that I was ignoring her.
I've been busy, you know, you know that I've been very busy.
With all these articles I've had to write.
My diary has been full to the brim.

Derrick: I need you to do something for me, well, for you, to help yourself.

Julie: I hadn't told her that, I didn't tell her because we hadn't seen each other.
So, I thought it would only be polite if I said hello.

Derrick: Now I think we have developed some form of trust?
Wouldn't you say?

Julie: I went over and the curtains were pulled shut.

Derrick: A bond?

Julie: Strange to have your curtains shut at 8am.
Especially in summer, with all that nature outside.

Derrick: I can feel it.

Julie: I knocked on the door.
No answer.

Derrick: I need you to film your sessions with Stephen.

Julie: So I knocked again, louder this time.
Still, no answer.

Derrick: I want you to film yourself.

Julie: Then the door opened.

Derrick: I want you to understand something.

Julie: It must have been the wind, joint with the force of my knocking.

Derrick: You do want help don't you?

David: Yes.

Julie: Her cat walked towards me.
Its tail, waving.
It looked thin.

Derrick: Take this camera and we will watch it together the next time we meet.
We'll go from there.

David takes the camera
He explores the camera with great detail

Julie: I started to call her.
"Hello"

I said.
No answer.

Derrick: OK?

David turns on the camera and begins to film the room around him

Julie: Why would you leave your door open?
You know what this street is like, don't you?
Look what happened to her a few months back?

Derrick: David?

Julie: She must be ill.

David: OK.

David begins to set the camera up
He puts the camera on a tri pod in the corner of the room
He is very specific, he wants the footage to be perfect

Julie: People only close their curtains and stay in bed at 8am if they're ill.

Derrick: Shall we put the lock on the safe?

Julie: I am making her a pie.
I have bought all the ingredients.
I'll take it over tomorrow morning.

Derrick: End the session there?

Julie: The lights are still off.
The curtains are still shut.
Twelve hours later.

Derrick: I just want to help.

Four.

The camera is filming the session
The live footage is projected onto a screen or a blank surface

Stephen: The whole lot?

A screech

Derrick: Six down.
Starts with 'C.'

A screech

Julie: They are doing it again.

David: I was fascinated by matches.

Always have been.
It's the noise.
The striking sound.
Does it for me.

A screech

Julie: Hark!
Louder than before.
Can you hear them?

David: I used to steal them from the kitchen drawer.

Julie: Derrick!
They are calling.

	They sound close don't they?

                    They sound close don't they?
                    Don't you think?

Derrick: That's the wind.

Julie: No it isn't.
Oh, I'm afraid.

A screech

Julie: Again, hark!

David: I take them up stairs and hide them underneath the pillow.

Julie: You can't say that's the wind.

David: When I went to bed, I'd take them out and strike them on the wall.

Derrick: Ok, that wasn't.

Julie: They are very, what's the word?

A screech

Julie: Bold.

Derrick: That's not right.

Julie: Ferocious.
What do you think they are calling for?

Stephen: Did you enjoy the fire too?
The match bursting into flames?

A screech

Julie: Hark!
Even louder than before.
They sound close.

Derrick: That's the echo.
It makes them sound closer.
They must be mating.
It's mating season.

That's a mating call.

Julie: Is it?

Derrick: It is.

A screech

David: One day Mum was out and I was playing with them.
I was thirteen.
I don't know what happened, I went for a shit.
When I came back, my fucking bedroom was on fire.
So, I try to piss on it, right?

Julie: It sounds as though they are in pain.
That noise does not attract.

David: It didn't go out.

Derrick: She is desperate.
The males are drawn in.

David: I remember running out the house, and hiding behind a car.

Julie: It sounds as though they're being attacked.
Abused.
Come here Derrick.

Stephen: So, we're looking up at the house burning.

Julie: Look!
Over there.

David: Huge flames burning, high.

The heat was –

Julie: They're rumbling through the rubbish.

David: And the smoke was –

Derrick: Trying to find something they can sink their teeth into.

Julie: The filthy felines.

Derrick: Foxes are dogs.
Apart of the dog family.

Julie: They have ears like cats.

Derrick: Foxes are dogs.

Julie: They have claws like cats.
They have the hair of a cat Derrick.

They have the eyes of a cat.

A screech

Julie: Look at them going through them bins!
If we didn't have that ban on bloody fox hunting, this wouldn't happen.
There would be less of them.

Derrick: Animal cruelty Julie.
You could understand their argument.

Julie: You shouldn't have too much of something Derrick.
Look what happened to those Nazis.

Derrick: I know Julie.
I was only saying that their argument was convincing.
Even I started doubting.

Julie: You did not.

Derrick: I did.

Julie: I feel like I don't know you anymore Derrick.
You have always been stubborn.

Derrick: There should be more room for change in this day and age.

Julie: You've always been like your Father, never like you Mother.
Set in your ways Derrick.

A screech

Julie: The door is locked isn't it?

Derrick: The door?

Julie: Yes, the door.
We saw that documentary about the twins.
The foxes broke in and they went upstairs and tore those babies' faces off.
So, yes, the door, is it locked?

Derrick: I'll go and check.

Julie: Take the bat.

Derrick takes out a baseball bat from underneath the mattress
He exits

Stephen: And what do I do?

David: You weep.
On the floor.

First, you drive up to the house, you see the blaze, the fire.

You stop the car.
You open the boot.
You take out a blanket and you lay it on the street, and then, you weep.

A screech

David: I hide behind a car.

Julie: Derrick?

Stephen: Don't you come out?

Julie: Derrick?

David: Yes, eventually, but not straight away.

Julie: DERRICK.

Derrick: Yes?

Julie: —

Make me a cup of tea while you're down there.

David: I want you to understand it was an accident.

I'm going to come up behind you, and I will hug you from behind.

I will kiss you on the cheek and I will hold you, tight.

You will tell me everything will be fine and you will tell me, it wasn't my fault.

Five.

Derrick: There's no milk.

Julie: There is, we went shopping.
We bought a pint yesterday.

Derrick: We seem to have used it.
It's gone.
We did put it in the fridge?

Julie: Yes, we always put it in there.
How strange.

Derrick: We never use more than half a pint in a day.
Did you have some cereal this morning?

Julie: Did you look in the drawer, at the bottom of the fridge?

Derrick: Yes, I looked in the fridge, on the top of the fridge, around the fridge and in the drawer.
There is none.

Julie: We must have used it all.

Derrick: Did you have cereal this morning?

Julie: Yes, I had one bowl.

Derrick: Just one?

Julie: I'm positive.

Derrick: Was Linda here today?

Julie: Yes.

Derrick: Her usual is around eleven, isn't it?
She visits around eleven?

Julie: Around that time yes, but today, it was nine.

Derrick: She's feeling better then?

Julie: She must be.

Derrick: You never asked how she was?

Julie: No.

Derrick: Why not?
You knew she was unwell.

Julie: Well, she looked well enough.
And, she came around at nine when it's usually eleven.
She made us a banana cake, to say thank you for the card.

Derrick: Card?
We didn't send her a card.

Julie: No, we didn't.
I gave her a card

Derrick: Did you?
You never told me we were sending cards?

Julie: We always send cards.

Derrick: Yes, for Christmas, Birthdays, but we've never sent a 'Get well soon' card.

Julie: It wasn't a 'Get well soon' card it was a 'Thinking of you' card.

Derrick: Were you?
Were you thinking of her?

Julie: Of course I was, we are friends.

Derrick: Are you sure?

Julie: Positive.

Derrick: Did you thank her for the banana cake?

Julie: She didn't know, I don't like banana cake.

Derrick: You do like bananas.

Julie: I do like bananas, but I don't like banana cake.
It's odd.

Derrick: Did you have coffee or tea?

Julie: Linda has it black.

Derrick: I said did you?

A cat

Derrick: Is that a cat?

A cat

Derrick: Julie, there is a cat in our house.

Julie: There isn't a cat in our house.

Derrick: I can hear it.

A cat

Derrick: You see, a cat!

Julie: I found it in the park.
It was hurt.

Derrick: You stole a cat?
You stole a cat out of the park and brought it home?

Julie: I have put it in the wardrobe.
It was hurt, it needed my help.

Derrick peaks into the wardrobe

Derrick: Is that Linda's cat?

Julie: Yes.

It needed somewhere to go.
Linda couldn't keep it.
Linda is ill.
She couldn't look after it.

Derrick: You said Linda looked fine.
You said she was well.

Julie: I did not say she was well.
She finds it hard to walk.

Derrick: She is not disabled.

Julie: She could have broken her leg.

Derrick: Julie, Linda has sprained her ankle.

Julie: The poor woman.
She is in pain.
The very least we can do right now, is take care of her cat until she recovers.

Derrick: She made us a cake.

Julie: She put her love into that cake.
It was overflowing with gratitude.
Don't be so bloody ungrateful.

Derrick: Ungrateful!
You told her you don't like banana cake.

Julie: Are you suggesting that I should lie to her?
That's all the poor woman needs.
A broken leg and a friend that lies to her.

She borrowed some of our milk to make another cake.
An apple pie this time.
I like apple pie.

	To say thank you for the card I sent her.
Derrick:	It was Linda? Linda used up the milk.
Julie:	And the cat. It needed a drink. Now, I'm going to sleep. Good night.

A cat

Julie:	- It hates me Derrick. It doesn't come near me. It keeps its distance and it stares, at me, it glares. I can tell it hates me.
Derrick:	It's frightened. New house. Trapped inside of a wardrobe. Living in a room with people it's never met. I would be.
Julie:	It's met me before. It knows me, it just doesn't like me. I've stopped feeding it cat food.

A mouse

Derrick:	What's that?

Julie: What's what?

A mouse

Derrick: That!

Julie: We have mice.

Derrick: When did we get mice?

Julie: Today, I bought them.
Six.

Derrick: You bought mice?

Julie: Yes, for the cat to play with.
I wanted to see how it would react.

Derrick: Are you are trying to win it over?

Julie: I want it to feel comfortable.

A mouse

Derrick: What about me?
I don't feel comfortable.
I come home and I want to put my feet up.
I don't want mice whizzing underneath them.
They have to go.

Julie: They will go.
Soon.

Derrick: When the things are devoured!

Julie: They are mice.
Alexandra needs to play.
Alexandra needs to be entertained.

Derrick: Bollocks!
What if they breed?
Make a little bed inside of our furniture?
What if they give birth to over thousands of little mice?

Julie: We won't let that happen.
Alexandra will catch them before that happens.

Derrick: Will you stop calling it that.

Julie: It's her name.

David: There is only one more situation.

Mum had a lot of men, when Dad left, when he went away, Mum needed comforting.

She'd go out a lot.
She'd bring men home and shag them.
Every morning there would be a different man in the kitchen.

Then she got married.

David begins to take his clothes off and then he folds them, neatly

When she was asleep, her husband would
come into my bedroom and get into bed
with me.
He'd put his arm around my waste and his
lips around my ear.

He'd suck it.

I'd pretend I was asleep.

He became obsessed with me.
He'd buy me anything I wanted.
Fags, vodka.
On my twelfth birthday, he bought me a
porn mag.

I'd sometimes rip my favorite girls out and
I'd talk to them and imagine they were
answering back.
I'd chat them up.
I'd get them into bed and spunk on their
chests.
In my head, that is.

I didn't say anything about him to Mum,
until after the fire.

I should have.

David is now in his underpants

A year later, I started to go out, around
town, Rotherham, Barsnley, Donny.
You could do that at my age back then.
I'd fuck three girls a week.

The toilets in the club had to do, or Rose hill.
It was dark and sometimes I could go bareback, the girls were too drunk to notice.
Twelve girls a month.

One hundred and forty four a year.
For about three years.
-
I want to be him, to play him.
I want to feel what he felt.
I'd like to understand.

I'd like to sleep at night, knowing I killed a dangerous man.
A man that could have potentially fucked my life up.
I don't want to stay awake at night thinking I killed a man that needed love, from another man.

I didn't know he was asleep.
I didn't even know he was in the house.
I thought he was at work.

David gets into his position

Stephen: I'll miss you.

David: You don't say that.

             You shouldn't say that.

Stephen: I will though, just so you know.

	I think we should kiss, to say goodbye.

David: I'm not going to do that.

Stephen: It's the proper way to say good bye.

David: You're mental.

Stephen: I know.

David: You should get yourself seen to.

They laugh

David: I bought you something.
To say thanks.

David gives Stephen a wrapped gift

David: So, here you are, thanks.

Stephen opens it, it is vests, a pack of three

Stephen: I followed you, last week, when you left here.
I wanted to see her.
Your girlfriend.
I wanted to see how you were, around her.

I wanted to see what she looked like.
So I followed you, to a house.

A nice house, with really nice windows.
You walked in through the side door.
I got closer, peaked through.

I thought you might have looked at me once, but you didn't see me.

And then it began.

She was younger than I thought she would be.
She was very pretty.

I saw you lick her dry.
And then you fucked her.
From behind, no eye contact.
You had your eyes closed all the way through.
You looked as if you were in pain for a little while.

And then, when you shot your load, you left.

When you left, your girlfriend sat on the floor naked and she began to cry.
Stroking her bump.
You never mentioned she was pregnant.
You didn't tell me that.

I came back here, and I sat there, and I thought about it, a lot.

You were wrong, you know.

I had what you've got.

I was sorted before that accident.
I was fine.

I had a great relationship with my parents.
I had a job that I loved.
I was engaged.

Then, the car crash.
Then the operation.

Apparently when I woke up, I was 'Unrecognizable.'
That's what my Dad said.

I became frustrated.
I became aggressive.
Pissed off.
Savage.
Pushed everybody away.
I was out of control.
I lost everything.

I would cherish what you have David.

Love your girlfriend and make her your wife.
Love you baby.
Take care of your Mum and enjoy your job.
Because I would do anything to have what you do.

I should have died.
I didn't want that heart.
You said it was full of love.
It wasn't.
You were wrong.

Friday Night

Julie:
>Broad beans and runner bean and peas in a pod.
>Proper mash that's freshly made,
>With a fillet of cod.
>That's Friday night for us, a treat we enjoy.

Stephen:
>Two day old Chinky that's been left on the floor.
>Pro-per-ly scraping out the noodles makes more.
>That's Friday night for me and maybe a boy.

David:
Double click and double click and double click some more.
Double click and double click searching hardcore.
>That's Friday night for me,
>Until it gets sore.

Derrick:
>Sometimes I sit alone with my guitar to end the day,
>And I recall a Swinton song my granny used to play.
>It starts in e and ends in b but the words are hard to say,
>For the word pronunciation is done the Swinton way.

>>It goes, Yang, tang tethera,
>>Meth-er–a–riff bip basara,
>>Says-a-rack-e–er, Con-dera, dick.

>>It goes, Yang, tang tethera
>>Meth-er –a –riff bip basara
>>Says- a- rack-e –er , Con-dera, dick.

The following verses are to be sung simultaneously

Julie:
>Broad beans and runner bean and peas in a pod.
>Proper mash that's freshly made
>With a fillet of cod.
>
>That's Friday night for me, a treat I enjoy.

David:
>My girlfriend makes dinner, last night she made duck,
>She poured on the peaking sauce when I'd rather fuck.
>
>That's Friday night for me, until I get bored

Stephen:
>Double dick and double dick my clients adore.
>Double dick and double dick my clients want more.
>
>>That's Friday night for me
>>Until it gets sore.

Derrick:
>I click and double click to help with the song,
>Tick tock and click clock the evening goes on
>That's Friday night for me
>Alone with my thoughts

Six.

Julie: She wasn't interested in the slightest.
You could tell.
After she left yesterday, I had a little think to myself.
I thought there could be a small possibility, it could've been me.
Maybe, it was because I wasn't interesting enough.

Derrick: I find you very intelligent.
All those books you read.
The research you do.

Julie: I am very intriguing.
But maybe, this very particular conversation, I wasn't, perhaps my tone was wrong.

Derrick: There is nothing wrong with your voice.

Julie: It is possible that, this particular conversation, my tone was uninteresting.
You know?
I sometimes blurt on and on.
I believe I saw her mind drifting, she looked, out the window, I remember.

Derrick: I'm sure you have nothing to worry about.

Julie: I tried to ring her, did she pick up?
No she didn't.
Probably thought I would bore her again.

Derrick: You are not boring.
She could be out.

Julie: Out where?

She thinks we're boring.
She believes we lack character and personality.
I bet that's it.
We need, we need to do something.
Right.
From now on, we only eat Mediterranean food.

We live in one of those, routines.
Those dull, unexciting things.

Routine, routine, ROUTINE, FUCKING ROUTINE.
We need to do something.

We may as well be dead!
I feel dead!

I was sorting the wardrobe out today and you have three pairs of brown shoes.
Three pairs of brown shoes!
I don't know anybody with three pairs of the same shoes.

We need to do something.
Anything.
Something exciting.
I've always wanted to be a ballet dancer, ever since I was a little girl.

Derrick: You're forty-two!

Julie: I'm taking dance classes Derrick.
Starting tomorrow.

Derrick: Where are you going?

Julie: I am going to The Trumpet Bar.
Linda recommended it ages ago.
But I said I didn't like brass.
I don't listen to brass.
How can I dislike something I haven't tried?
We've never been there.
I'm going to do ballet on the dance floor.

Derrick: You're going to do ballet, in a Trumpet Bar?

Julie: And tap Derrick.
And maybe, I will do Jazz.

Derrick: I'll get my coat.

Julie: It isn't your thing Derrick.
You don't like trumpets.

Derrick: I do like brass.

Julie: No, you like a big brass band.
But it's not a band.
It's just trumpets.

Derrick: I think trumpets are cool.

Julie: They are Derrick, very cool.
They are going to be playing in the cool bar.
But, trust me Derrick.
You won't enjoy it.

Derrick: Ok then, I'll lay here and finish my cross word, wait for you to get back.

Julie: Don't wait up too late.
I've plans to stay out until dawn.

Derrick: You won't stay out that late?

Julie: You only live once Derrick.

Derrick: You've never been the 'Stay up late' type.
You've always been the 'Bed for nine' type.

Julie: People change.
Tonight I am saying yes to everything I would have normally said no to.
I'm doing shots.
Squashed Frogs?
I think that's what they're called.
Or is it squashed dogs?
I'll tell you all about it tomorrow.
Oh nearly forgot the key.
Have a nice night Derrick.

Derrick: Right.
Got it.

Derrick writes

I'm gunna say yes

Julie:

> Tonight I'm gunna say yes.
> Tonight I'm a born again virgin.
> Tonight Mathew I'm going to be Miss Chief.
>
> I'll do class A drugs,
> End up in a cell,
> So, at W.I I'll have a story to tell.
> Yes, my night will be swell,
> For tonight, I say yes.
>
> Risk my health for the sake of yes!
> Find myself out in a club.
> Fuck it! I'll have flaming Sambuca.
> And I'll burn my lip but I just won't care,
> And in the ladies I'll shave myself bare.
> Let down my hair!
> I'm gunna say yes.
> Yes.
> Yes!
> Yes!
> YES!
> 'I'm coming out of my cage and I'm doing just fine'
> Now I'm losing my way so I'm gunna say yes!
> Yes.
> Yes.
> Yes!
> Yes!
> YES.
> YES!
> I'm going to say YES!

Seven.

David: It's getting cold again.

I needed a walk.

Derrick: Fancy that.

Winter will be on its way soon.

David: Autumn, winter, it's the same.

You were seen 'Eradicating the grounds' you know.
A lady, a woman walking her dog.
Came up to me and told me you were digging back there.
Digging holes.

Derrick: My cat died.

David: Shit.

Derrick: Julie went to the CO-OP.
Came home to find the cat, laying in the living room, blood everywhere.

Julie made us get one of those CCTV's a while back, she said it was protection.
We watched it back, it was awful.
We saw the poor bleeder get torn to shreds by one of those foxes.

David: Fuck.
Where's the wife now?

Derrick: She's out.
The Trumpet Bar.

David: And you chose to bury your cat instead?

Derrick: I don't think she finds me very interesting anymore.
I think she believes we have very little in common.
She believes I don't have a sense of humor.

Some nights, I come home from work, eat my dinner and then we sit on the sofa.
Watching programs, programs that don't really interest me, but I watch them.
The sort of programs that you don't think about afterwards.
Programs that you forget about the next day.
Pointless television programs.
They don't interest me, but I watch them, because she enjoys them.

Sometimes I laugh, erratically at the screen, to show her that I do have a sense of humor.

We used to fuck.
Several times a week.
We used to make love two times a week.
Now we sit there.
Not touching, not holding hands.
By nine were in bed and we turn off the bedside lamp on the bedside table and we turn away from each other.

And she sleeps.

I stay awake and try to make sense of things.

Last year for our anniversary, I bought her Sunset Boulevard on DVD.
It was the first film we ever watched together, on our first date.

She told me that she had already seen the film, and didn't like it much.

She cried.
On our first date, at the end of the film, she cried.
And when she cried, I knew right then that I found her very beautiful.
She has always been so very beautiful.

We haven't had sex with each other in five months.
We haven't kissed each other in three weeks.

She asked me, a couple of months back, she asked me
"Why don't we fuck anymore?"
And I didn't reply.
I couldn't.
I pretended I didn't hear her and I carried on with my crossword.

It dangles there, it is attached, but it feels nothing.

| | It swings from side to side, a dead piece of skin.
They call it impotence.

I took a tablet once, two of them.
You know, the tablets from those machines in the rest rooms.
Four pounds for two tablets, and I took them both and thought about her vagina.

I didn't throb once.
It didn't twitch.
No movement what so ever.

I haven't told her.
I can't.
I don't know how to.

I don't suppose you've seen my wife? |
|---|---|
| **David:** | I don't know, I don't think so. |
| **Derrick:** | How much would it cost for you to fuck her?

How much would it cost?
How much would I have to pay? |
| **David:** | I'm not going to fuck your wife. |
| **Derrick:** | She's a beautiful woman David.
One hundred pounds?
Two hundred?

We can keep it between us, two friends. |

David: I don't want to.

Derrick: Beautiful ass.
She will treat you right.
She has a beautiful pussy too.

Tight and wet.
You like them tight don't you?

David: I don't want to.

Derrick: Fuck her in the ass.

David: I won't.

Derrick: She is very intelligent, my wife.
Have I told you what she does for a living?

She works for The Sun.
Freelance.
She's been asked to write this article on domestic abuse.
Apparently it's really current.
Very now.

She says everybody is hunting for the biggest story.
All the papers are fighting for it.
The editors are salivating over the very thought of it.

She told me she is keeping her eyes and ears open.
They've all been told that.
To be aware.

She will look after you don't worry.

You're very handsome.

Handsome man like you deserves to be treat right you know.

David: I can't.

Eight.

Bedroom light on

Julie: I want you to fuck me Derrick.

Derrick: What time is it?

Julie: Four.
I want you to fuck me, and I want you to pull my hair, hard.

Derrick: Julie.

Julie: Pull my fucking hair.

Derrick: Your scalp would bleed.

Julie: I want you to lick it.
My vagina.
Clean it out with your tongue.
And then you will fuck me.

Derrick: I can't.

Julie: You won't.
You won't because you don't want to.

Derrick: I want to –

Julie: I want to hit you Derrick, I want to hurt you with my thumping.
I want you to grab me by the arms and I want to struggle as you force me down onto the bed.

| | I need you to fuck me. |

Derrick: I can't.

Julie: You don't love me.
You haven't for a while.

Tonight, I stood on the dance floor.
Swaying from side to side.
You know?
Like I used to.

A man came.
Not particularly good looking, but I was taking anything.
He stood behind me and he started to gyrate.
That's what you call it?
Isn't it?
When a man rubs his hard penis against the arse cheeks?

He took me back to a hotel room.
Premier Inn?
It was very clean.
The floor was very clean.
He took off my dress and then the man stopped, he paused and he admired me.
He told me I was elegant.
He said I looked magnificent.
Beautiful.
You don't think I'm beautiful.

Derrick: I do.
You are.

Julie: Then fuck me.
Show me, if you think I'm beautiful, then show me.
I want you to stick it in me Derrick.
I want you to cum inside me, and I want you to look into my eyes as you do it.
Shoot deep into my throbbing vagina.

Derrick: Shall I lick it?
You want me to lick it?

Derrick gets down onto his knees
Julie grabs his hair

A screech

Julie throws him onto the bed

A mouse

She climbs on top of him
Julie pulls down Derrick's pants and starts to pull on his cock
Like a ravenous teenager
Needing it

Derrick: Julie.

Julie: Give it to me.
Show me you fucker.

Julie groans a deep frustrated grunt
Desperate for penetration
She pulls it harder, then harder and the pull turns into a hit and then a thump

She begins to hit and thump Derrick erratically

Julie: You shit, fuck, fucking twat.
Fucking prick!
Fucking cunt!
Cunt!
CUNT!
SHOW ME!

A screech

Derrick: Stop this.

A screech

Derrick takes her wrists and throws her off the bed

Another mouse

Derrick: I need you to stop this and I need you to listen.

Julie takes the baseball bat

Derrick: Is this what you want?

Julie swings it
Mice
She misses

Derrick: Listen.

She swings
Mice
She misses

Derrick: Is this what you really –

She swings again
She hits Derrick
A screech
Derrick falls to the ground

She swings again
She hits Derrick
A screech

She swings again
Derrick manages to grab the bat, they struggle
They fall to the ground, they struggle, both holding onto the bat
Derrick climbs on top of Julie
Derrick manages to snatch the bat off of Julie
He throws it, it smashes into the main light in the bedroom, plunging the bedroom into darkness

The mice invade

We hear Derrick and Julie struggle further
A screech

Derrick tries to restrain her
A screech

THUMP
Silence

When the bedroom table lamp is turned on, we see that Julie is now handcuffed to the bed

Derrick: I need you to understand something.

You're afraid I understand that, I am too.
But sometimes we need to barge past that
fear and just say something.

The past is unchangeable but the present
is an opportunity.

We need to fill in the cracks of the past,
bush away that dark glow and cease that
opportunity.
Create what we can with the remains of
what we have.

David enters

Derrick: We need to love generously, do anything and give anything.
Live selflessly.

David kneels and takes out his wallet

Derrick: We can design a palace with a pile of rubble.

David takes out the photo of his father and him playing baseball

Derrick: We can be happy.
Out there, is true inhabitable glee, all we need to do –

David takes out a pack of matches from his pocket

Derrick: All we need to do –

David strikes a match

Derrick: All we have to do –

David moves it closer to the photograph

Derrick: Is dig.

Darkness

END.